OTHER CHILDREN´S BOOKS BY CARL-JOHAN FORSSÉN EHRLIN

The Tractor Who Wants to Fall Asleep – A New Way of Getting Children to Sleep
(Ehrlin Publishing, 2017)

The Little Elephant Who Wants to Fall Asleep – A New Way of Getting Children to Sleep
(Penguin Random House, 2016)

The Rabbit Who Wants to Fall Asleep – A New Way of Getting Children to Sleep
(Penguin Random House, 2014)

Title: Brave Morris – A Week Upside Down
Originally published in Sweden as *Modiga Morris – en vecka upp och ner*, 2018
Text and illustrations copyright © Carl-Johan Forssén Ehrlin and Ehrlin Publishing AB, 2019

English translation copyright © Tara Chace, 2018
Illustrations and design by Katarina Vintrafors
Author photography © Jonas Nygren

Paperback ISBN: 978-91-88375-23-0

www.carl-johan.com
www.ehrlinpublishing.com

Brave Morris
A WEEK UPSIDE DOWN

CARL-JOHAN FORSSÉN EHRLIN

ILLUSTRATED BY KATARINA VINTRAFORS

Translation by Tara Chace

e.

EHRLIN PUBLISHING

FOREWORD

The idea of watching helplessly as a child cries or is in pain is very difficult, especially as a parent. Depending on the circumstances, children are sometimes happy, sometimes sad, and sometimes everything is just upside down. My hope is that this innovative book will provide both the child and you as a grown-up the tools to manage different situations that come up in everyday life.

With Brave Morris' help, I want to suggest what we can achieve by changing our thinking and present techniques that can be used in similar situations for children. Reading this book several times, will help the child be more and more open to giving these approaches a try in similar situations. As a grown-up, you can then refer back to the book and how Morris dealt with something. It may motivate the child to make use of these effective techniques in order to make a change.

Brave Morris' experiences can also serve as the basis for conversations while you read. You can talk about feelings such as pain, loss, fear, kindness, and joy. At the end of the book, I give examples of how you can apply the techniques described in the stories. If you want to get the most out of this book, I recommend that you read through these tips before you read the stories to your child.

The techniques used in the book have been drawn from various coaching techniques, psychology, and my own experiences working with people as a coach and teacher over the past twenty years. I'm also the father of two children, and I'm constantly trying to improve at helping them. These techniques are tested and have helped not only my children but also many thousands of people all over the world. It is my hope that they will also help the child you are reading this book to.

Good luck!

Carl-Johan Forssén Ehrlin

Morris lives with his mom, dad, and big sister Molly. They just moved, and Morris has brought all of his things to their new home.

Morris is a brave, curious boy who is usually happy and likes to have fun. He likes to discover things and play with his sister and his friends. He likes climbing trees and especially hanging upside down from the branches.

Sometimes when he's put things into his pockets, they fall out onto the ground when he's hanging upside down in the trees.

He likes riding his bike but has a little trouble keeping his balance, and sometimes he falls. Then he tries again. Morris is determined.

When Morris grows up, he wants to be a police officer, a teacher, an astronaut, or maybe a doctor. He hasn't made up his mind.

He wonders what it would be like helping other people or flying in space. Morris wants to do so many things.

There are many exciting things to discover in the new town—playgrounds, climbing trees, and new friends. But never would Morris have imagined that his first week would be so upside down.

MONDAY

When Morris wakes up, he has a worried feeling in his stomach. Tomorrow he is supposed to start at a new preschool. Morris wonders if he'll make some new friends there. He likes his old friends, of course, but they're still back in the town Morris' family moved from. What if Morris will be all alone now? The more he thinks about it, the more worried he becomes until, finally, he starts to cry.

His big sister Molly hears that Morris is upset.

"How are you doing, Morris?" Molly asks.

"I'm worried, and I don't like feeling this way," Morris says.

"Why are you worried?"

"I don't know if I'll make any new friends to play with at preschool. Can you help me feel happy again?"

"Of course I can. I'm the best in the world at making you happy!" Molly says.

"Think about it this way! Every feeling actually spins around inside your body like a merry-go-round. Sometimes they even go outside of your body. If you want to change one feeling into a different feeling, you can change how the feeling is spinning. You can even play with a feeling so much, both inside and outside your body, that it gets confused and disappears."

Molly waves her arms in the air, showing how feelings can move around.

"Try it with your feeling, and you'll see!" she says.

Morris is curious and tries it out.

"It starts here," he says, pointing at his body, "but then it changes direction and spins the other way instead. Look, Molly! It's going around like a racing car at full speed. Now it's heading out of the room and out of the house and into the street."

Morris lets his worried feeling move around in every possible direction until he can't feel it anymore. Now he has a giggly feeling in his stomach instead and starts laughing.

"I knew I could get you into a good mood," Molly says. "Tomorrow is a new day, and I know you'll make a lot of new friends."

TUESDAY

Today is Morris' first day at his new preschool. Dad stays for a while in the morning, and everything feels good. But then Dad has to go to work.

There are three teachers at preschool and plenty of kids Morris can play with. They're all nice to him. Even so, he can't stop thinking about his friends at his old preschool. Morris starts to cry. He misses them.

A teacher sits down next to him.

"Hi, Morris. How are you doing?" the teacher asks.

"I'm sad. I miss my old friends."

"I understand that you miss them. It's totally OK to feel that way. Do you want to try something with me that might help you?" the teacher asks.

Morris is curious. He wonders what the teacher is talking about.

"Do this: Pretend you have a picture of your friends somewhere in front of you. Can you see the picture? Where is it?"

Morris points in front of him and says, "Right there!"

"Good! Now, you're going to move the picture. Pretend you grab the picture, pull it into your heart, and then save it there. Now, your friends will always be with you in your heart, no matter where you are."

Morris does what his teacher suggests and saves the picture in his heart. He feels warm and happy when he thinks about his old friends.

His teacher says, "Now, pretend you see a new picture in the same spot in front of you. It's a picture of you and your new friends at this preschool. Look at you and your friends playing together and having fun."

Morris spends a while watching the imaginary picture he's thinking about now. Then he stands up and says, "I'm going to play with my new friends now!"

The day passes quickly. When Morris' parents come to pick him up, he tells them how much fun he's had and how many new friends he's already made. Morris can't wait for tomorrow when he can come back to preschool and play with them some more.

WEDNESDAY

Morris had a fun day at preschool. All the kids spent almost the entire day outside. Morris did some digging in the sandbpit, rode a bike, and played with his new friends. They pretended they were animals, and Morris was crawling around on the ground like a worm. When his mum came to pick him up, he was really dirty.

When they get home, his mum says, "Time for a bath!"

She fills the tub with water and a lot of bubbles. Morris jumps in. He splashes around in the water with his boats and rubber ducks, making the suds swirl high. He's a pirate and the king of the sea!

Suddenly he notices a spider on the wall and gets scared. He quickly moves to the other end of the tub.

"Mum!" Morris calls.

"What's up?" his mum asks.

"There's an icky spider on the wall! There!" Morris says, pointing.
"That little thing?" his mum asks.

Mum tells him that the spider's name is Tina. Then, she starts telling a story: "Once upon a time there was a spider named Tina who came to visit her grand-mother. The spider grandmother gave her eight red socks that she had knit. She said Tina could wear them if it got cold outside. 'But remember to lend the socks to your friends if they're cold too,' the spider grandmother said. Tina was happy and also borrowed grandmother's old orange hat. With the hat and socks on, Tina the little spider felt so happy that she danced the whole way home. Tina often wore the socks and hat, but just as her grandmother instructed, she was happy to loan them to her friends."

"Morris, can you tell if Tina is wearing the red socks and the orange hat today? Or has she lent them to a sibling or a friend?"

Confused, Morris looks at his mum and then at the spider.

"No, Mum. I don't see any socks or a hat. Tina must have lent them out today."

Mum laughs and asks, "Did you know that Tina the Spider likes to dance when you sing to her? Let's see if she'll dance for us!"

They sing "Itsy Bitsy Spider" and do the hand motions with it. At the same time, they pretend the spider is happy and dancing.

Tina climbs up the wall and dances into a little crevice. Morris isn't afraid of Tina anymore—and not of any other spiders, either. Instead, the they feel like Morris' friends.

THURSDAY

In the morning, Dad is walking Morris to preschool. Morris is happy, running around chasing some butterflies that have just woken up.

Suddenly he stumbles and scrapes his knee, causing a small scrape. It throbs and hurts. Morris starts crying, but Dad comforts him and says,

"I understand that it hurts. But did you know you can make your knee hurt less or even make the pain go away?"

Curious, Morris looks at his dad as tears run down his cheeks.

"Do you see that woman riding her bike over there?" Dad asks.

"Yes," Morris says with a sniffle.

"Well, let's put the part that hurts onto the bike so it will be gone when the woman rides away," Dad says. "What colour is the pain you're feeling?"

"Red!" Morris says.

"If it could make a noise, what do you think it would sound like?"

"It says ow!" Morris says firmly.

"Good! And what shape does the pain have?"

"It looks like a football."

"So, a red football that says ow?" Dad asks.

"Yes," Morris says, feeling calmer. "But it still hurts, Dad."

"It will go away really soon," Dad says reassuringly. "I want you to take the red ball and put it on that bike." He points at the bike as the woman rides away.

"Now that she's riding away, the part that hurts will go with her and disappear altogether in a just a moment. Plus, your scrape will heal faster and faster the farther away she rides."

Morris watches the bike. He pretends the red ball of pain starts bouncing toward it. Every time the ball bounces, it yells "Ow! Ow! Ow!"

The ball bounces all the way over to the bike. It lands in the bicycle basket just as the woman rides out of view, far away.

"It's working, Dad!" Morris calls. "The pain is almost totally gone, and I feel my scrape starting to heal already!" Morris dries his tears and takes Dad's hand. Together they walk the rest of the way to preschool.

During the day, Morris tells his friends how Dad helped him get rid of the pain when he hurt himself. He shows the scrape that's healing faster and faster.

FRIDAY

It's time for lunch at preschool. Morris is hungry.

Sometimes Morris decides that he doesn't like certain foods. Today, he doesn't like broccoli. Morris doesn't want to eat, even though he's hungry and actually can't remember why he doesn't like broccoli.

"I don't like broccoli," Morris tells one of his teachers.

"That's too bad," she says. "Are you hungry?"

"Yes, I am."

"Have you ever said or thought that you didn't like something but then discovered that you actually liked it?" his teacher asks with curiosity.

"Well . . . this one time I was at the zoo with Dad, and we were going to eat. And he bought pasta with shrimp. I said, 'I don't like shrimp!' But Dad got me to try it anyway, and I thought it was good. Now I always eat shrimp."

"Great! Can you think of any other times when that happened?"

"This other time I was super hungry, but Mum only had a banana. I didn't like bananas, but I tried it anyway. I ate the whole banana and thought it was delicious!" Morris said proudly.

"Plus, there was this time I got mushrooms in my soup," he continued eagerly, "it almost made me throw up. I really thought mushrooms were disgusting! But when I tasted it, it was really good."

"So, several times when you tried something, you ended up liking it. I'm sure that will happen in the future, too! Maybe even right now?" his teacher asks.

Morris eyes the broccoli on his plate with curiosity. He's going to be brave and try a bite. He slowly puts some broccoli in his mouth and starts chewing. He is quiet and focused. What does it actually taste like? Mushrooms? Shrimp? Maybe both—or like a banana? He smiles at his teacher and takes another bite with his fork. Morris is happy. He has discovered he likes broccoli.

When Morris comes home, he tells his parents how he learned to eat broccoli at preschool and how brave he was. At dinner, he asks to have broccoli again.

Morris had a fun day with his sister Molly. They did some baking, skipping and rode their bikes. He thought the best part was when they did the baking. Molly spilled a lot of flour, which turned her face all white like a ghost's. Everyone laughed at that, even Molly. But now the day is over and it's time for Morris to go to bed. Mum turns off the light, and the room gets darker. Morris feels scared.

"I don't like it when it's all dark and black," Morris says.

Mum thinks for a while and says, "Have you ever thought about how black is just a colour?"

"What do you mean?"

"Well, your clothes and toys come in different colours, right?"

Morris nods and says, "Yeah, that's true."

"When it gets dark in here, all of the things in the room just change colours. Everything else is still just like it was when the lights were on. If you want, you can pretend that everything in the room is turning a different colour instead. Black could turn into blue, yellow, or any colour you want. Maybe your favorite colour? When it gets dark, you can let your mind think of all kinds of fun things and let go of everything else."

Mum continues, "Even if the room gets dark at first when the lights are switched off, after a while your eyes will adjust. Then you'll often be able to see a little more, even if the colours are slightly different than during the day. When the light was on you couldn't see the stars in the sky outside your window. It's only when it's dark enough that you can see the stars!"

"The stars are so pretty, Mom!" Morris says.

"So, if I adjust to the dark, I can look at the stars while I fall asleep?" Morris asks.

"Yes, you can. You can do that every night," his mother says, tucking him in.

"Then I want to learn to like the dark," Morris says.

Mum starts to sing "Twinkle, Twinkle Little Star" while Morris gets settled in bed and looks at the stars. He´s trying to count them, but his eyelids grow heavier and heavier. And just before his eyes close and Morris falls asleep, he whispers, "I'm not afraid of the dark anymore."

Mum kisses Morris on the forehead and says, "You're so brave. Good night, wonderful child."

SUNDAY

Morris wakes up feeling extra happy. His family is going to the park today to play on the climbing frame and swings and have a good time together. He hurries out of bed and makes sure everyone else in his family is awake and getting ready to go.

There are a lot of people playing together at the park, both kids and parents. Morris likes climbing, and he climbs way up high on one of the climbing frames. Then he hears another child crying. A little boy is sitting at the very top of the climbing frame.

"Why are you crying?" Morris asks him.

"I'm scared and I can't climb back down," the boy says.

Morris has an idea. Maybe he can change how the boy feels, the same way Molly helped him. He decides to give it a try.

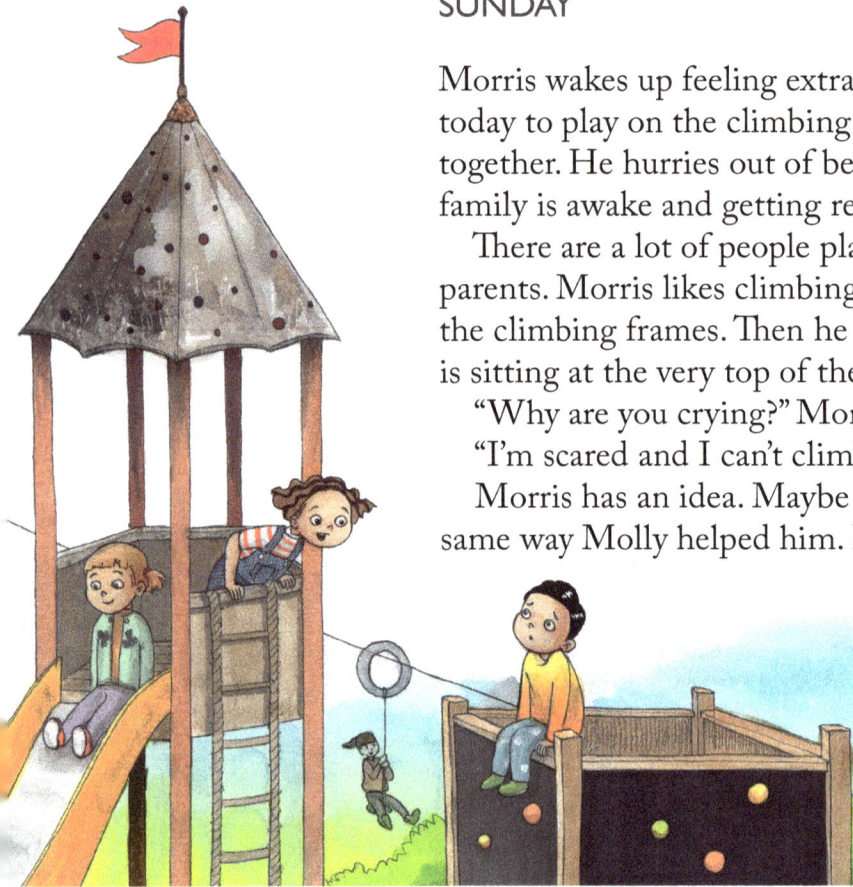

"Pretend that you take the scared feeling and spin it the other direction in your body. Or pretend it flies up into space!" Morris says.

"I'll try," the boy says, imagining for a moment. "Oh, it works!"

They climb down together. The little boy is so happy. Morris feels proud that he was able to help.

Next, Morris walks over to the swings. There's a girl sitting there, who's afraid of a spider. Morris decides to help her, too. He asks,

"Is the spider wearing red socks and an orange hat?"

"Uh, no," the girl says, confused. "Spiders don't wear socks or hats, do they?" she says.

"Then maybe she's lent them to a friend," says Morris and keeps playing. The girl looks at him confused but then starts to laugh. She starts swinging again without caring about the spider. She feels safe and happy again.

When Dad and Morris are climbing on a climbing frame, Dad falls and hits his leg. It hurts a lot. Morris helps him get rid of the pain the same way Dad helped Morris when he fell.

Morris asks what colour the pain is, what it sounds like, and how it looks. Dad answers and soon he feels better. He gives Morris a hug and says,

"Thanks for your help, Morris! The pain in my leg is almost completely gone. You've learned so much during this sometimes upside-down week. You are brave little kid. I wonder who you'll help tomorrow? Let's go have our picnic now. We can eat the cake you and Molly baked yesterday."

TIPS FOR USING THE BOOK

In this part of the book, you as a grown-up can learn more about the techniques that Morris learns and how you can use them to help a child who finds her- or himself in similar situations. First, I'll share some general tips that are good to bear in mind when you're communicating. Next, I'll describe the techniques that Morris learns day by day and give examples of how you can put them into practice.

From my many years of experience as a coach and educator, I am convinced that the techniques I describe actually work with the majority of children and grown-ups. Some techniques work better with some children than with others and they may sometimes need to be repeated a few times before they become a natural method for dealing with challenging situations. Some children immediately adopt the techniques and they become a natural part of their everyday lives. Other children want to talk about the techniques Morris learns and test them several times before they believe in them. Neither way is right or wrong; they are just different ways of absorbing new skills. Have patience and keep believing in the techniques, and convey this to the child.

Sometimes the child doesn't want to listen to the whole story but would rather talk about something that happened on a certain day, and about her or his own experiences and feelings in similar situations. Take time to discuss the child's feelings, and continue reading another time. The intention of this book is to open up a dialogue with the child and plant the idea of being able to do something about difficult situations by looking at them in a different way. I hope you can apply the situations described in the book as teaching tools.

The book describes situations based on a classic nuclear family with a mother, father, and two children. You can freely modify the text to match the child's family situation, no matter what it is. For example, "Dad" can become an uncle or grandfather, and "Mum" can become a sister or grandmother.

THE EFFECT OF ONE'S OWN BEHAVIOR

To convince the child to believe in the techniques that Morris uses in the book, you yourself must believe in them, or really give the book's unlimited potential a chance, and then convey this to the child. This is when the magic happens. As a grown-up, you have an incredibly important job as a role model for the child. If you are afraid of a (harmless) spider when the child sees it, the child will quickly learn to be afraid of spiders as well. This is why you may need to practice self-awareness and examine how you behave yourself in similar situations to truly succeed in using this book. So long as you as a grown-up show the child that you are calm and you believe the story, the magic of the book will take root in the child.

MENTAL MAP

All people experience the world differently. This is why there is no universal reality that everyone can relate to; we all live in different "worlds." Our interpretation of reality is shaped by experience, knowledge, culture, and many other factors that affect how we experience the world. The basis of our mental map is formed when we are young, and it effects our decisions even when we grow up. To help the child, we may sometimes need to set aside our own mental maps and the thoughts and assessments that we ourselves see as truths. If as a grown-up you believe that changes really are easy to make, the changes will happen. As long as we grown-ups think it is easy, it will become easier for the child. Keep an open mind, and help the child as best you can. If you can convey the techniques in the book convincingly, it will help the child throughout her or his life.

DIFFERENT SENSES THAT DOMINATE

Just as we adults learn in a variety of ways, children also have a variety of sensory strengths that affect their learning. Some will understand references to vision better, others to hearing, and still others to touch. This is why the techniques in the book vary and use different senses to stimulate a child's learning in the best way. This means that certain techniques will probably appeal to the child more than others do. As a grown-up, it is good to observe what works best for the child and try to engage with the child in a similar way in other situations, too. If you are creative, you can find new techniques that use the sense or senses that the child best responds to. Keep an open mind, and have fun together—the change that you both seek will follow.

BREAKING MINDSETS

Sometimes you can get stuck in a certain frame of mind or thinking in a way that keeps you from solving a problem. The purpose of the situations that Morris encounters and how he manages them is to show the power of thinking in a new way when in vulnerable situations. Only then can you change your view of the situation and change how you experience things. By using symbols, colours, and movements, you can creatively break old thought patterns, making the brain more receptive to new ideas and feelings. When you try the techniques in everyday life, you will help the child break her or his negative mindset, which will make it possible for the child to feel better.

MONDAY

Anxiety about joining a new group

Description of the technique
Emotions that we feel can be thought of as spinning around in parts or all of our bodies, and even outside of ourselves. There is no right or wrong—all people represent and symbolize feelings differently. When it comes to Morris' anxiety, his sister helps him redirect his feeling as well as stick to more positive feelings while they are playing with the anxiety. By changing the direction of the feeling and how it is moving, the consciousness gets disoriented and becomes receptive to new feelings.

Something to think about
You can have the child imagine that feelings are spinning inside, in and out of the body, or maybe sometimes they bounce along or hit a wall and speed back into the body if necessary so that the new positive feeling will grow strong. Test what works best, and have fun.

Example
Sometimes I feel motion sick when I travel by plane or ride on a merry-go-round. When I stop and explore how I feel, it feels distinctly like my motion sickness is moving around inside of me. On those occasions, I have fun changing the direction it's spinning, and this immediately helps calm the sensation in my body.

TUESDAY

Missing friends

Description of the technique
As human beings, we tend to look in the same direction with our eyes on repeated occasions when we think back on a particular memory. When we think about something that we like, our eyes look in one direction, and when we think about something we don't like, our eyes usually look in a different direction. What is happening is that we are looking at mental images we have "placed" there. The mental images represent those memories and feelings. Our subconscious creates these images and places them outside of ourselves. We are actually looking at the mental images right in front of us. By becoming conscious of this, we can train ourselves to consciously shift mental images and, in that way, make big changes about how we feel. In the story, Morris receives guidance from a teacher in replacing the image of playing with his old friends, inserting a new image in the same place. In the new image, Morris sees himself playing with his new friends. This speeds up an internal change.

Something to think about
If you want to use this technique with a child, it is important that you not block the child's field of vision when you ask her or him to picture something, because you will prevent the child from seeing the image. Instead, position yourself to the side and look in the same direction, and maybe point to where the child's image will be. Then, engage to reinforce the child's experience of that image. If the child doesn't see an image, ask her or him to pretend to see it, and then the child will form an image.

Example
I have used this technique countless times to help grown-ups make big changes in their lives. One of the most common reasons is to strengthen self-confidence. Once someone visualizes a situation or person symbolizing safety, he or she can then visualize his or her own self-esteem. If the images have turned up in a variety of places, in other words the client has been looking in different directions, I have helped him or her move the images of themselves on their own to a place that symbolizes safety. Suddenly the client stretches, and an inner change has begun, which will help the person to unconsciously connect him- or herself with the self-confident person and believe in him- or herself more.

WEDNESDAY

Fear of spiders

Description of the technique
The fear of spiders is common and can sometimes develop into a phobia. In some cases, it's a legitimate fear because there are actually spiders that are venomous and even deadly. Despite the fact that venomous spiders are relatively uncommon in most parts of the world, though, we still sometimes experience an incorrect and excessive fear of these small creatures. It is an instinct from far back in time when our ancestors lived among many dangerous animals. In the story, Morris is scared of a spider. Together with his mother, he changes his fear by altering the association he has with spiders.

Something to think about
It is often relatively easy to help a child with this kind of technique as long as you focus on shifting the association to something positive, and with a positive intention. With this technique, you can be creative and have fun together. It is beneficial if you manage to involve the child in coming up with ideas on her or his own about how to think about the spider. Ask questions: What do you think the spider likes to do when she's not at preschool? Do you think she likes playing soccer with her spider friends? Do you think her football goal is made out of cobweb?

Example
Many clients have come to me with a fear of spiders, and together we have created new associations for spiders by having the client change the mental image of the spider. Have them put on a silly hat, or wool socks, or a clown nose. For stronger phobias, I have also had them play a mental video forward and backward where they change how they would act if they saw a spider in the movie. If you also have them imagine silly music during the movie, it's even easier to make a change. In most cases, it is enough to change the image of a spider to dispel the fear, especially in children who have an easy time using their imaginations.

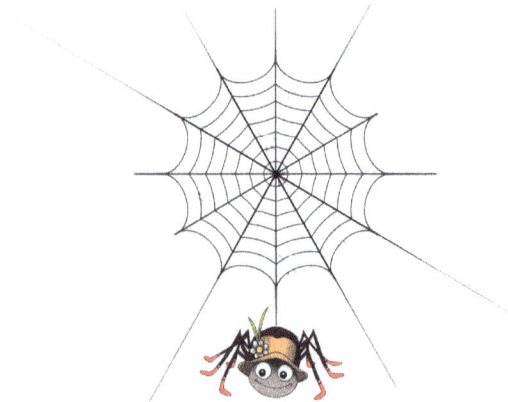

THURSDAY

Getting hurt

Description of the technique
Morris falls on the way to preschool and hurts himself. To help Morris cope with the pain, Dad asks him to assign a colour, shape, and sound to it. By imagining the pain as an object, your brain starts to distance itself from the pain and reduce it. In the book, Dad asks Morris to take the thing that symbolizes the pain and send it away on a bicycle that's moving away from them. In this way, the brain will dis-tance itself even more from the experience of the pain, further reducing it.

Something to think about
Involve as many senses as possible when you ask the child to describe the pain, and repeat what the child brings up. The more real you can make the symbol of the experience of the pain, or whatever other emotion you want to change, the more the brain will believe it and accept the change that occurs when the object is sent away.

Example
The first time I used this technique on my oldest son was at a restaurant when he was three years old. He had pinched his finger and started to scream in pain. I immediately adopted this technique to help him. "What colour is the pain?" I asked. "Red," he replied. We continued by describing the pain and then threw it into a flowerpot farther away. He calmed down and continued eating his food. After that incident, it became easier and easier to use the technique with him whenever something happens because he had learned what to do.

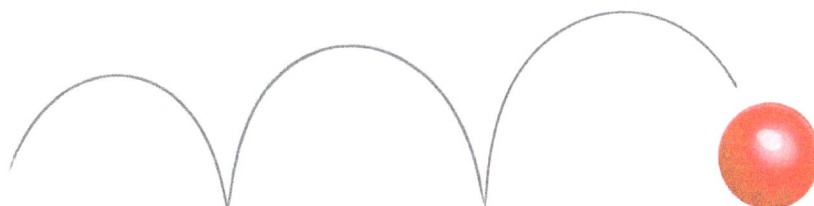

Refusing food

Description of the technique
Our brains love to generalize things. If we burn ourselves once on a stove, we will be afraid of burning ourselves on any stove for a long time to come if we do not change that association. Children often get hung up on something being wrong with the food—it was served wrong, foods were touching each other, or whatever the problem was—and they continue to generalize these views until convinced otherwise. One way to break this attitude is to get the brain to focus enough on the desired way of thinking by providing enough examples to start generalizing the positive instead.

Something to think about
Try to get the child to come up with examples by asking leading questions. If the child doesn't come up with anything, help out by asking about different situations that you are familiar with. Try to come up with three to four examples or more, which will reinforce the desired behavior or mindset. Avoid negative examples that might lead to bad generalizations.

Example
As children, we sometimes need to hear that we are good enough the way we are. If the child is looking for confirmation of this from a grown-up but doesn't get it, the child will start generalizing that the problem must lie with her or him, and the child will start to doubt her- or himself for a while. This behavior often continues into adulthood, and I've coached a lot of adults who never started believing in themselves because of a repeated lack of confirmation in their childhoods. To turn around this kind of self-assessment in an adult, we do exactly the same thing as with Morris, who started thinking of enough positive memories and was able to transform a negative mindset into a positive one instead.

SATURDAY

Fear of the dark

Description of the technique
Morris is afraid of the dark and doesn't like it when his mother turns off the light. This situation can be utilized beneficially as part of a wider perspective on teaching the child to deal with the dark in other contexts. Morris' mother helps him change his mind about what darkness means. She plays down the dark by having him think of it as just a colour and then helping him focus on the positive aspects of the dark, which here means being able to see the stars better.

Something to think about
As grown-ups, we can help children use their good imaginations to see the world differently when something scares them. As long as we as grown-ups believe in what we want to convey, the child will be more willing to try out what we suggest.

Example
I remember a situation when I was giving my son a bath. For some reason, the power went out, and the whole bathroom went completely dark until our eyes started to adjust. My son reacted and began to feel anxious. I kept my calm and talked with him about darkness as a colour, just as in the book. He started talking about things that are black, and after a while our eyes started to adjust, and we could see more and more of the room. Suddenly the power came back, and the lights turned on. This was the first time he suddenly ended up in the dark, and my approach as a parent kept him from creating a negative association with the dark.

SUNDAY

A day in the park

Description of the technique
Sunday is a positive day when everything is going Morris' way, and he starts to use his new skills to help other children as well as his own father. This day in the story is intended to remind the child about what has happened previously and, at the same time, reinforce the skills from the other days by showing how they can be used in other contexts with other children—and even with grown-ups.

Something to think about
Since the intention of the book is to sow a seed about what you can do to mitigate everyday problems when they arise, this Sunday story reflects how you can work with the child to keep these new insights alive. By using everyday conversations with the child to tie back into things that happen in the book, the child will be able to hang on to what she or he has learned, and when similar problems arise, like the ones Morris faces, the child will be more willing to try the techniques and, hopefully, be helped by them. A good idea is to refer to the book when needed: Do you remember when Morris fell and hurt himself?

Example
In our everyday lives, I routinely talk with my oldest son, reminding him of things that he has done before. I mention situations when his behavior paid off. Maybe he noticed another child crying and wanted to go over and help the child or managed to go to the bathroom every time he needed to while potty-training. Experiences like these are reinforcing for him because they remind him of his successes. This will form the basis of his behavior for the rest of his life. The more times you think back on a memory, the easier it is to remember it again, and it will have a greater influence on your thoughts. Remember that.

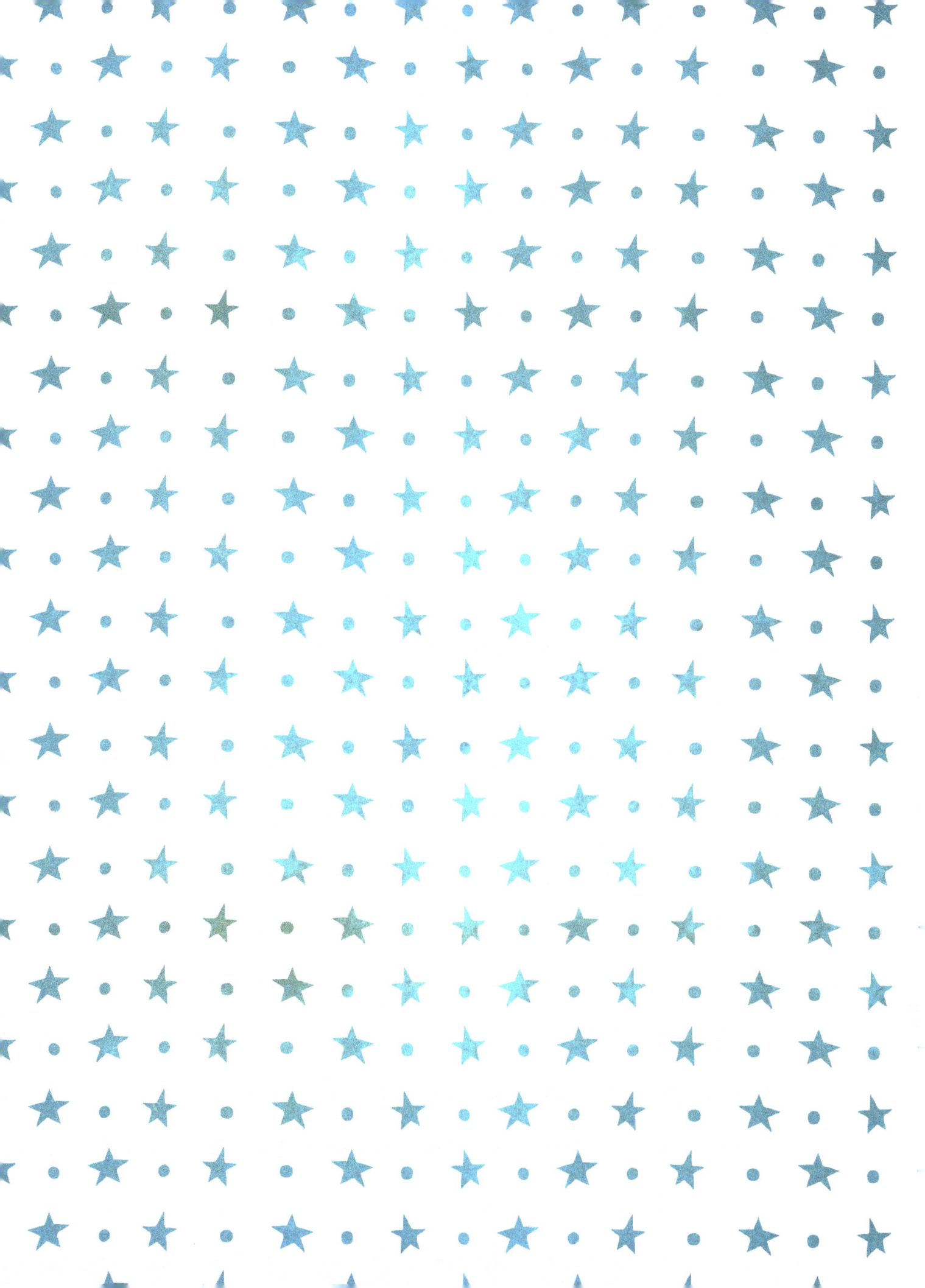

ABOUT THE AUTHOR

Carl-Johan Forssén Ehrlin had his breakthrough in 2015 with the children's book The Rabbit Who Wants to Fall Asleep. The book became a global phenomenon as the first self-published book to become a bestseller on Amazon. Thanks to satisfied parents talking to their friends about the book and writing about it in social media, the book's magic has spread all over the world and today has sold several million copies.

Carl-Johan Forssén Ehrlin is trained as a behavioural scientist with a Bachelor's degree in psychology and is a certified NLP Master Practitioner. He has worked for many years as one of Sweden's foremost coaches, lecturer and educator in leadership, communication and personal development. Carl-Johan occasionally teaches at the Jonkoping University in Sweden and also gets requests from universities around the world. Today he primarily works with writing and publishing his books on leadership, personal development and books which help children.

Read more about Carl-Johan at www.carl-johan.com.

Photo © Jonas Nygren

www.ingramcontent.com/pod-product-compliance
Lightning Source LLC
Chambersburg PA
CBHW060901090426
42738CB00025B/3491

9 789188 375230